The BIG, BIG FEELINGS
ACTIVITY BOOK

beaming books
MINNEAPOLIS

29 28 27 26 25 24 23   1 2 3 4 5 6 7 8 9

Paperback ISBN: 978-1-5064-9190-5
eBook ISBN: 978-1-5064-9191-2

63474; 9781506491905; FEB2023

Beaming Books
PO Box 1209
Minneapolis, MN 55440-1209
Beamingbooks.com

Everyone has emotions! But what are they? Emotions are strong feelings, like love or anger or fear, often accompanied by a physical reaction. So when someone is happy, they're usually smiling. A frown or crying could show that someone is sad.

How do we handle our emotions? The first step is to identify them. And then we can learn how to manage our emotions, and our physical responses, so that we're expressing our feelings in a healthy way.

What do you do with BIG feelings?

This activity book can help you identify, understand, and use creative ways to work through those big emotions.

COLOR ASSOCIATION

Match each color in column A with the emotion we often associate it with in column B. One has already been done for you.

- -

Column A	Column B
Red	Happy
Blue	Angry
Green	Afraid
Yellow	Sad
Orange	Embarrassed
Pink	Jealous

Answer key found on page 62.

DRAW YOUR BIG EMOTIONS

Using the space below, draw something that makes you feel angry.

_ _

BRAINSTORM!

What helps you feel better when you're angry?

— — — — — — — — — — — — — — — — — — — —

— — — — — — — — — — — — — — — — — — — —

— — — — — — — — — — — — — — — — — — — —

— — — — — — — — — — — — — — — — — — — —

— — — — — — — — — — — — — — — — — — — —

— — — — — — — — — — — — — — — — — — — —

— — — — — — — — — — — — — — — — — — — —

— — — — — — — — — — — — — — — — — — — —

HOW CAN YOU . . .

help a friend who is angry?

_ _ _ _ _ _ _ _ _ _ _ _ _ _ _ _ _ _ _

_ _ _ _ _ _ _ _ _ _ _ _ _ _ _ _ _ _ _

_ _ _ _ _ _ _ _ _ _ _ _ _ _ _ _ _ _ _

_ _ _ _ _ _ _ _ _ _ _ _ _ _ _ _ _ _ _

_ _ _ _ _ _ _ _ _ _ _ _ _ _ _ _ _ _ _

_ _ _ _ _ _ _ _ _ _ _ _ _ _ _ _ _ _ _

_ _ _ _ _ _ _ _ _ _ _ _ _ _ _ _ _ _ _

_ _ _ _ _ _ _ _ _ _ _ _ _ _ _ _ _ _ _

BREATHING EXERCISE

When feeling angry, try focusing on your breath to calm down. Take a slow, deep breath in on the count of 1 . . . 2 . . . 3 and then a slow, deep breath out for 1 . . . 2 . . . 3. Repeat. Next, try breathing in for four counts and breathing out for four counts. Repeat. Hopefully you're starting to feel calmer and in control of your emotions.

WALK IT OUT!

When emotions are overwhelming, sometimes taking a walk helps. Ask an adult for permission. Walk around your yard or neighborhood. What do you notice? Write down what you see, hear, and smell. Now think about how you feel. Has your mood changed?

_ _

_ _

_ _

_ _

_ _

_ _

_ _

ACROSTIC POEM

This is a poem where the first letter of each line spells out a word. Using each letter below as your starting point, create your own poem about emotions.

E _____

M _____

O _____

T _____

I _____

O _____

N _____

S _____

WORD SEARCH

```
X  N  E  R  V  O  U  S  H  X  K
F  H  A  I  J  V  T  U  A  L  A
B  R  Z  L  E  Q  C  O  P  E  N
E  K  U  Y  M  A  D  L  P  M  X
X  W  B  S  O  K  G  A  Y  W  I
C  M  P  A  T  N  S  E  Q  O  E
I  D  F  D  I  R  F  J  F  R  T
T  Q  L  G  O  T  A  N  G  R  Y
E  R  U  X  N  S  B  T  Y  I  V
D  M  T  E  P  K  O  H  E  E  Z
A  W  J  Y  S  C  A  R  E  D  I
```

Emotions	Sad	Scared	Worried
Frustrated	Angry	Excited	Jealous
Mad	Happy	Nervous	Anxiety

Answer key found on page 62.

CRUMPLE ART

If you're feeling angry and need to release that emotion, try making crumple art. Take a blank piece of paper. Crumple it up. Now open up the crumpled paper. Can you make something beautiful out of the wrinkles and creases in the paper? See what you can create!

BRAINSTORM!

What helps you feel better when you're sad?

_ _

_ _

_ _

_ _

_ _

_ _

_ _

_ _

_ _

DRAW YOUR BIG EMOTIONS

Using the space below, draw something that makes you feel sad.

— — — — — — — — — — — — — — — — — — —

HOW CAN YOU . . .

help a friend who is sad?

_ _

_ _

_ _

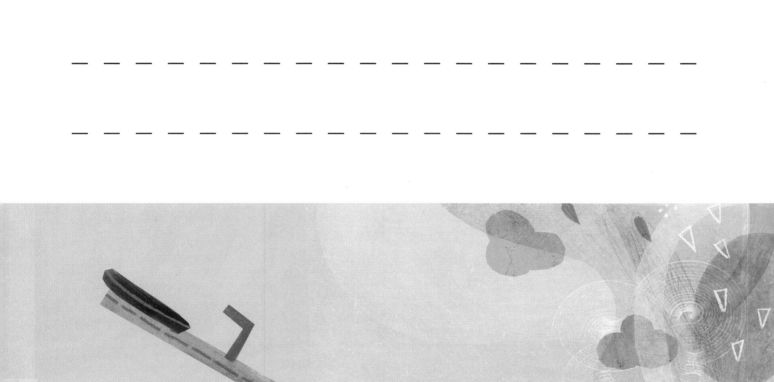

EMOTIONS BINGO

Create your own bingo card by filling in each blank square below with an emotion. Using objects from home, like pennies or old buttons, mark off each emotion you feel during the day. At the end of the day, are you surprised by how many different emotions you marked?

Start the bingo card over each day to see how your feelings change from day to day. Or try leaving the markers in place and using a different marker each day of the week to see how your emotions change!

CONDUCT AN INTERVIEW

Using the questions below, interview a trusted adult about how they manage their emotions. You may find some new ideas that work for you!

— —

When they are sad, they _____

_____ .

If they feel scared, they can _____

_____ .

Some things that help them feel better when they're mad are

_____

_____ .

One thing that always makes them laugh is _____

_____ .

BE A TREE!

Movement can help release emotions. Stand tall like a tree. With your feet stationary, twist your arms back and forth with your upper body. Focus on your breath. Feel the wind against your arms and think about letting your emotions float off into the air.

LAUGH IT OUT!

Laughter is a great way to help improve or change our mood. Can you figure out the punch line to these jokes?

— —

1. What does Santa suffer from if he gets stuck in a chimney?

2. Why are frogs always happy?

3. Knock, knock! Who's there? Boo. Boo who?

4. Did you hear about the angry pancake?

5. Why was the baby strawberry crying?

6. What do you call an emotional marshmallow?

7. What do you call an angry dessert?

Answer key found on page 63.

WORD SCRAMBLE!

Unscramble each word below.

– –

raneg _____   nidk _____

rateh **h**_____   inemoto _____

elowly _____   glinefe _____

halug _____   lebu _____

radaif _____   yahev _____

Answer key found on page 63.

DRAW YOUR BIG EMOTIONS

Using the space below, draw something that makes you feel happy.

— —

BRAINSTORM!

What people, events, or activities make you happy?

_ _

_ _

_ _

_ _

_ _

_ _

HOW CAN YOU . . .

spread happiness to others?

_ _ _ _ _ _ _ _ _ _ _ _ _ _ _

_ _ _ _ _ _ _ _ _ _ _ _ _ _ _

_ _ _ _ _ _ _ _ _ _ _ _ _ _ _

_ _ _ _ _ _ _ _ _ _ _ _ _ _ _

_ _ _ _ _ _ _ _ _ _ _ _ _ _ _

_ _ _ _ _ _ _ _ _ _ _ _ _ _ _

_ _ _ _ _ _ _ _ _ _ _ _ _ _ _

_ _ _ _ _ _ _ _ _ _ _ _ _ _ _

KINDNESS ROCKS!

- -

YOU WILL NEED:

- medium-size rocks
- water
- small paintbrush
- paints
- clear sealant

- -

1. Look around your yard or neighborhood for medium-size rocks.
   Gather rocks (check with an adult first to make sure it's okay).
2. Wash the rocks off with water if necessary to remove any dirt.
3. Using your paintbrush and paints, create a different design on each rock.
4. Let them sit in the sun to dry.
5. Cover each painted rock with the clear sealant (ask an adult to help).
6. Give painted rocks to friends or family, or leave them in places around
   your neighborhood for others to spot!

DANCE IT OUT!

Take a dance break. Turn on a song and dance out your emotions!

— —

DRAW EACH EGG A FACE

Draw a face on the egg to correspond with the emotion listed below.

- -

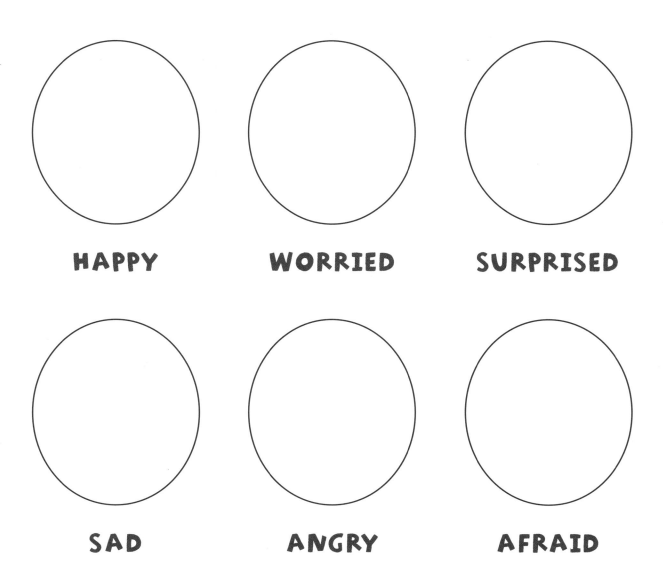

HAPPY   WORRIED   SURPRISED

SAD   ANGRY   AFRAID

DRAW YOUR BIG EMOTIONS

Using the space below, draw something that makes you feel afraid.

— —

BRAINSTORM!

Write down what helps you feel better when you're afraid.

_ _

_ _

_ _

_ _

_ _

_ _

_ _

_ _

HOW CAN YOU . . .

help someone else who is feeling afraid?

‒ ‒

‒ ‒

‒ ‒

‒ ‒

‒ ‒

‒ ‒

‒ ‒

‒ ‒

CREATE A CALMING SPOT

- -

Pick a spot in your house or room where you can go when feelings are overwhelming. Make this a dedicated area, with items that can help you feel better. Here are a few ideas:

- blankets
- pillows
- stuffed animals
- drawing materials
- favorite books

- -

If you're feeling too many emotions, go to your calming spot. Get comfortable. Read or draw or write to help refocus your mind. Let yourself calm down and reset. When you're feeling better, leave your calming spot ready for the next time you need it.

GROUND YOURSELF WITH THE FIVE SENSES

Sometimes it's hard to focus when you're experiencing different emotions. One way to try to calm down is to take a deep breath and think about the five senses:

— — — — — — — — — — — — — — — — — — —

Close your eyes.

What do you hear? _____.

What do you smell? _____.

Now open your eyes.

What do you see? _____.

What do you taste? _____.

What do you feel? _____.

PHYSICAL FEELINGS

Sometimes we feel our feelings through our body, such as crying when we're sad. Using a different color for each emotion, draw where you physically feel each feeling on the outline of the body below.

– –

SAD

ANGRY

EMBARRASSED

AFRAID

CREATE YOUR OWN STRESS BALL

YOU WILL NEED:

- a balloon
- a funnel
- filling material (small dry beans, lentils, rice, or birdseed)

1. Blow up the balloon to stretch it out. Deflate before you start.
2. Pull the balloon over the small end of the funnel.
3. Carefully pour in your filling material.
4. Tie the balloon closed.

Now try it out!
Squeezing a stress ball can help you relax when you're feeling overwhelmed with emotions.

ACROSTIC POEM

This is a poem where the first letter of each line spells out a word. Using each letter below as your starting point, create your own poem about feelings.

F _____

E _____

E _____

L _____

I _____

N _____

G _____

S _____

BALLOON BREATHING

You can do this exercise sitting or standing. Pretend your stomach is a balloon. Take a deep breath in through your nose to make the balloon bigger.

Then breathe out through your mouth. As you breathe out, purse your lips like you're blowing bubbles.

PHYSICAL RESPONSES TO EMOTIONS

Use the following list and check off any physical responses you've experienced. What emotion did they accompany?

- -

☐ Stomachache   ☐ Clenched fists

☐ Crying   ☐ Hiding

☐ Heart racing   ☐ Biting your nails

☐ Frowning   ☐ Blushing

☐ Smiling

DRAW YOUR BIG EMOTIONS

Using the space below, draw something that makes you feel jealous.

– –

BRAINSTORM!

Write down a time someone else was jealous of you.

_ _

_ _

_ _

_ _

_ _

_ _

_ _

_ _

_ _

COLOR ME

HOW CAN YOU . . .

help someone else who is feeling jealous?

_ _

_ _

_ _

_ _

_ _

_ _

_ _

_ _

WHICH EMOTION?

Write down the emotion each face is showing.

- - - - - - - - - - - - - - - - - - - -

- - - - - - - - - - - - - - - - - - - -

Answer key found on page 64.

FINDING GRATITUDE

Whether we're having a good day or a bad day, it helps to remember what we're grateful for. Write down five things, people, or places in your life that make you feel grateful. Try to do this every day for a week and see your list grow!

1. _____

2. _____

3. _____

4. _____

5. _____

1. _____

2. _____

3. _____

4. _____

5. _____

THE BODY SCAN

Take a few moments to focus on what your body is feeling.

Sit or lie down on your back, and close your eyes. Focus on your breath, in and out.

Next, focus on your feet. Wiggle your toes. How do they feel?

Now focus on your legs. How do they feel? Relax your legs.

Move to your stomach. How does it feel? Take deep breaths as you mentally scan your stomach.

Now scan your chest. How do your lungs feel, breathing in and out?

How does your neck feel?

How does your head feel?

Now that the body scan is complete, do you feel calmer? Open your eyes, stand up, and try to keep that calm the rest of the day.

Whenever you're feeling angry or upset, a body scan can be a helpful way to regain control.

FEELINGS ALPHABET

Can you think of an emotion that starts with each letter of the alphabet? One has been done for you.

A _____   H _____

B _____   I _____

C _____   J _____

D _____   K _____

E _____   L _____

F _____   M _____

G _____   N _____

O _____

P _____

Q _____

R _____

S _____

T _____

U _____

V _____

W _____

X _____

Y ucky

Z _____

EMOTION CHARADES

- -

Two or more players.

Copy each word from the word bank onto a sheet of paper. Cut out each word. Place the papers in a container, like a cup or hat.

When it's your turn, pick a piece of paper. Demonstrate the emotion using facial expressions or body language—no talking! The other players will try to guess the emotion from your clues. Whoever guesses correctly is the next person to pick a piece of paper.

- -

WORD BANK:

Angry
Embarrassed
Sad
Nervous

Happy
Surprised
Worried
Scared

Silly
Excited
Jealous
Frustrated

SING IT OUT!

Singing is a great way to connect with and release emotions.
Turn on a favorite song.
If you know the words, sing along!

What do you like about this song?
How does it make you feel?
When the song is over, has your mood or emotion changed?

Try writing your own song lyrics to the same rhythm.

— — — — — — — — — — — — — — — — — —

— — — — — — — — — — — — — — — — — —

— — — — — — — — — — — — — — — — — —

— — — — — — — — — — — — — — — — — —

— — — — — — — — — — — — — — — — — —

52

BLOWING OUT CANDLES

Hold out one hand in front of your mouth. Each finger represents a candle. Wiggle each finger to represent a flame flickering. Using a long breath, try to blow out the "candles" one at a time. When a "candle" goes out, curl down that finger.

Focusing on your breath can help calm down those BIG emotions!

DRAW YOUR BIG EMOTIONS

Using the space below, draw something that makes you feel embarrassed.

_ _

BRAINSTORM!

What can help make an embarrassing situation better?

_ _ _ _ _ _ _ _ _ _ _ _ _ _ _ _ _ _ _ _

_ _ _ _ _ _ _ _ _ _ _ _ _ _ _ _ _ _ _ _

_ _ _ _ _ _ _ _ _ _ _ _ _ _ _ _ _ _ _ _

_ _ _ _ _ _ _ _ _ _ _ _ _ _ _ _ _ _ _ _

_ _ _ _ _ _ _ _ _ _ _ _ _ _ _ _ _ _ _ _

_ _ _ _ _ _ _ _ _ _ _ _ _ _ _ _ _ _ _ _

_ _ _ _ _ _ _ _ _ _ _ _ _ _ _ _ _ _ _ _

_ _ _ _ _ _ _ _ _ _ _ _ _ _ _ _ _ _ _ _

HOW CAN YOU . . .

help someone else who is feeling embarrassed?

_ _ _ _ _ _ _ _ _ _ _ _ _ _ _ _ _ _

_ _ _ _ _ _ _ _ _ _ _ _ _ _ _ _ _ _

_ _ _ _ _ _ _ _ _ _ _ _ _ _ _ _ _ _

_ _ _ _ _ _ _ _ _ _ _ _ _ _ _ _ _ _

_ _ _ _ _ _ _ _ _ _ _ _ _ _ _ _ _ _

_ _ _ _ _ _ _ _ _ _ _ _ _ _ _ _ _ _

_ _ _ _ _ _ _ _ _ _ _ _ _ _ _ _ _ _

_ _ _ _ _ _ _ _ _ _ _ _ _ _ _ _ _ _

HOW WOULD YOU FEEL IF . . .

– –

Everyone experiences some things that make them feel embarrassed. What might feel embarrassing to you may be no big deal to someone else, or the other way around. Color the faces next to each situation based on how you would feel.

BONUS: *Ask someone else how they would feel if it happened to them. Did they answer the same or differently than you?*

– –

Blue:	**PURPLE:**	**PINK:**
Not embarrassed.	*A little embarrassed.*	*Very embarrassed.*

- I forget to do my homework.

- I do not do as well as I wanted on a test.

- I spill a drink on my shirt.

- I make a loud noise, and everyone looks at me.

- I am speaking in front of the whole class.

- I trip and fall down in gym class.

- I have a bad hair day.

- I accidentally score a point for the wrong team.

AFFIRMATIONS

An affirmation is an act of saying or showing something that is positive and true. Fill out each sentence below to complete each statement about yourself in a truthful way. You can also ask a loved one to fill them out for you. Did you find any of the statements hard to complete? Are you surprised by traits your loved one sees in you?

— —

I believe in myself because _____

I am happy and healthy when _____

I am unique and special because _____

I am proud I can do _____

I show my strength when _____

I love when I _____

I have many talents, like _____

I can make a difference by _____

60

MOOD METER!

Using the mood meter below, plot your current emotion:

$-\ -$

Plot your emotions throughout the day. Is there an event or activity that made your mood change? At the end of the day, is your mood different from when you started the day?

Remember, all emotions are valid. We have feelings for a reason—even if we don't always like how we feel. There are ways we can help ourselves change our mood!

ANSWER KEY

COLOR ASSOCIATION/MATCHING

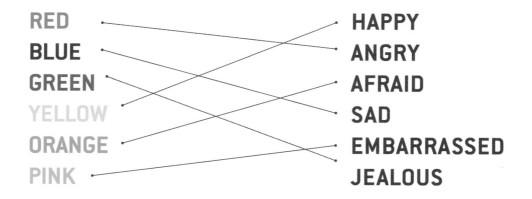

RED — SAD
BLUE — EMBARRASSED
GREEN — HAPPY
YELLOW — ANGRY
ORANGE — AFRAID
PINK — JEALOUS

WORD SEARCH